MW00936635

FOOTPRINTS to Land Records

A step-by-step guide to finding your grandparent's land.

FINALLY, A SIMPLE genealogy research guide to land records

By Donnis Slusser Crane

© 2012 by Donnis Crane

All Rights Reserved

No portion of this book may be copied, retransmitted, reposted, duplicated, or otherwise used without the express written approval of the author, except by reviewers who may quote brief excerpts in connection with a review.

Contents

Introduction

Research into land records is an essential part of the work of genealogy. Many genealogy researchers avoid county courthouses until a last resort. It is true that a great deal of historical land information is available on-line and more is being added every day. By all means, a person should take advantage of every available resource. **I wanted more!**

Some family researchers are satisfied with a visit to the grave of their ancestors. **I wanted more!**

I wanted to actually walk on the same land my ancestors walked. I wanted to see the things my great grandparents saw. I wanted to day dream about what their days must have been like and gain some understanding perhaps of how and why their decisions were made a certain way.

A visit to the community and to the actual land where my ancestors lived was a must for me. And my journey started with a trip to the county courthouse.

Chapter 1

Purpose of this Land Records Guide

The purpose of this guide is to aid the genealogy researcher in finding his/her ancestor's land records and land. It will help the researcher take the necessary steps:

- Starting with the government Census Records
- Visit to the appropriate county courthouse
    o Sift through the large number of records located there
    o Obtain a copy of the County Tract map
    o Get a copy of the Section land tract map
    o Search the Master Deed Index
    o Find the specific record
- Learn to read and understand deeds
- Map the route to their ancestor's land.
- Finally, go for a walk on that land.

This guide will SIMPLIFY, complement, and supplement historical texts. It is not a history book.

It is not the purpose of this guide to reprint all the historical information that is available through thousands of books and on line. Some history, however, needs to be understood for the sole purpose of recognizing the differences between the various types of governmental land survey systems.

First of all we must know that an address is NOT a land description; it simply tells where the property is located. A legal property description DESCRIBES THE LAND.

In this land records guide, you will learn the three main types of legal property descriptions and where they are used:

- The **Metes and Bounds system** which describes the land using geographical markers and length measurements.
- The **Rectangular Survey System** which uses Meridians, Base Lines, Townships, Ranges and Sections.
- The **Plat Map system** which uses Lots and Blocks in a contiguously improved acreage, called a development.

Chapter 2

The Original 13 Colonies

Long before the eastern seaboard of North America was populated by white immigrants, the common people in the old countries all over Europe dreamed of owning their own land. But there were obstacles and very few opportunities for them to rise above their existing financial stations.

When the first colonies in the new America were being settled England had the largest influence. To be profitable the colonies needed thousands of folks to settle on and work the land.

The King of England granted land to wealthy speculating companies, whose stockholders generally stayed in England and appointed land agents to act in their behalf in the new colonies. They authorized their agents to manage the company's land holdings, and bestowed the right to buy, sell and assign land rights from the company to individuals. The investors expected good land and property management and a return on their invested money.

The companies had to attract people willing to leave their homelands and travel to the new country. They tried to sell the land at first. Meanwhile, the common people were struggling with just feeding their families and had no extra money to buy land. Something had to be done. Not long after, the speculating companies began offering the land for 'free' to anyone who would be willing to settle there, invest some years of hard labor, and send all profits back to the company for a certain period of indenture. After that period, the company would then convey the land to the individual through a patent. The companies advertised all over Europe and when the people learned they could earn the ownership of the land through hard labor, they came to the new America.

Chapter 3

Metes and Bounds Survey System

Originally used in England, the Metes and Bounds description was brought to the Americas for use in the original 13 colonies, and continues to be used in those states today. The Metes and Bounds system of land records describes land using physical features of local geography, identifying markers, lengths, and directions. The descriptions frequently referred to adjoining properties and its owners. Every Metes and Bounds description must go back to where the beginning was, closing the description.

1. METES AND BOUNDS

"Beginning at the intersection of two stone walls near the apple tree on the north side of Muddy Creek road one mile above the junction of Muddy and Indian Creeks, north for 2 FURLONGS plus 3 RODS to the end of the stone wall bordering the road, thence northwest to the well on the corner of John Smith's place, thence west 400 FEET to the corner of a barn near a large oak tree, thence south to Muddy Creek road, thence down the side of the creek road back to the POINT OF BEGINNING." Consisting of 159.6 ACRES more or less.

This example of a Metes and Bounds legal description says: "Beginning at the intersection of the stone wall near the apple tree on the north side of Muddy Creek road one mile above the junction of Muddy and Indian Creeks, north for 2 **FURLONGS** plus 3 **RODS** to the end of the stone wall bordering the road, thence northwest to the well on the corner of John Smith's place, thence west

400 **FEET** to the corner of a barn near a large oak tree, thence south to Muddy Creek road, thence down the side of the creek road back to the **POINT OF BEGINNING.** Consisting of 159.6 **ACRES** more or less".

The Metes and Bounds system continues to use the early, old-fashioned language of the original descriptions. Because of the antiquated wording, it is usually difficult locating property in the states that continue to use the Metes and Bounds system of land descriptions. The legal descriptions don't typically contain information that is easily transferred to a current land map.

Many of today's measurement words were derived from the words historically used for farming. The length measurements were often expressed using old English vocabulary such as furlong, rod, poles, chains, etc.

A **rod or pole** is 5 ½ yards or 16 ½ feet.

Furlong was understood to mean the distance a team of oxen could plow without resting.

- It eventually came to be standardized to be 40 rods or 660 feet.

An **acre** used to mean the amount of land tillable by one man behind one ox in one day. Traditional acres were long and narrow due to the difficulty in turning the plow.

- One acre measured 40 rods (660 feet) long and 3 rods (49 ½ feet) wide.
- Today an acre is standardized as 43,560 square feet.

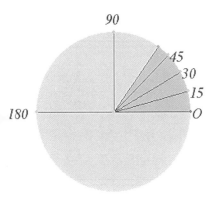

Sometimes the Metes and Bounds description will include 'courses' or directions that are not exactly true North, South, East or West, but instead a few degrees off North or off South or off East or off West.

A direction could be a true direction or it could use a compass bearing such as North 42⁰ degrees, 35′ minutes West which means slightly West of North.

Each survey shows the name of the individual for whom the tract was surveyed, the acreage, the courses and distances and the names of adjoining property owners, and other significant geographical features of the landscape like rivers, streams, hills, walls, trees, etc.

The endorsement "Returned" on the survey refers to the date the surveyor sent the survey to the Land Office to have a patent prepared. If the date of the patent itself is not known, the return date provides a useful starting point for patent searches.

Once a researcher finds the original land record, he must follow the sale of that land from the original date forward in time ending with the last, or current, land owner. For example starting with the original patent, to whom did this land owner sell the land, and then who did that person sell to, and then who did that person sell to, until you reach the final sale to the current land owner. The county property tax department can provide the location of the land based on the current owner's name.

The Metes and Bounds land descriptions have caused many discrepancies throughout the years. A good deal of the description frequently depends on people's traditions and memories of the local area. Among other things:

- Physical attributes of land are constantly changing. Trees get struck by lightning or chopped down. Streams and rivers can change course, dry up, or get dammed for use in flooding lakes.

- Towns get relocated, roads and county or state boundary lines could and did change over the years.
- Adjacent land owners could sell their land.

Discrepancies frequently led to law suits to resolve land ownership, and the courts were tasked with deciphering what landmark to which the original land surveyor was referring.

The Metes and Bounds Land Survey System is a difficult description to maintain. It is difficult locating property in the states that continue to use the Metes and Bounds system of land descriptions. Because the legal description has not changed since the land was first surveyed, the description does not easily transfer to a current land map.

Chapter 4

Rectangular Survey System

Following the Revolutionary War with England, the United States Continental Congress was deeply in debt.

uundary between Mississippi River and
th parallel uncertain due to misconception that
urce of Mississippi River lay further north

1775

They were fighting against governmental taxation without representation, so the new government had very little power to tax the people. Britain recognized American rights to the land south of the Great Lakes and west to the Mississippi River. The new federal government decided to sell the Territories west of the 3 original colonies to pay off the debt.

The problems encountered with the Metes and Bounds system caused the United States to look for a system to replace it. The Land Ordinance Act of 1785 was created to control the surveying, selling, granting, and settling of the new lands. With this new Public Land Survey system, (PLSS) also known as the Rectangular Survey system, land could be more easily identified.

The PLSS measures from a Meridian and a Base Line in approximate squares, creating townships and ranges. While the original 13 colonies and their derivatives kept their original Metes and Bounds land descriptions, most of the rest of the United States was surveyed into townships.

The government had initially set 640 acres as the minimum that could be purchased and the individual farmer could not afford to buy it. However companies and land speculators bought up huge tracts of land These speculators divided up the land and sold it off in smaller units: 160 acre tracts, 40 acres, sometimes as small as 20 acres which was affordable to more individuals. Initially, the land speculators made the money the government expected to make.

As the government gained more land through trades or purchases, it continued to sell it off encouraging settlers to move West. The government lowered the minimum required number of acres, sold land on credit and offered free land under a variety of different Acts. The U.S government has disposed of billions of acres of land as new territories were opened for settlement.

As the eastern states were becoming more crowded and available land more scarce, whenever a gateway wa discovered, surveyed, and opened, settlers spread West in search of a new beginning.

The first surveys under the new Rectangular Survey System (PLSS) were in eastern Ohio in an area called the Seven Ranges. The government was in a hurry to complete the surveys and get the land sold, resulting in considerable variances in shapes and sizes of townships. It remains that way to this day.

Moving westward, accuracy became more of a consideration than a rapid sale. The PLSS system was simplified by establishing one major meridian and one baseline per state. County lines often followed the survey, so there are many rectangular and/or square counties throughout the Midwest and Western states.

The PLSS system is used in some capacity in most of the country. For the exceptions check out Wikipedia. Search on Non-PLSS regions.

Legal ownership of land is recorded on documents found in the county courthouse where the land is located. This practice has resulted in safekeeping of millions of documents, stretching from today back to the very beginning of the colonies, and the original land patents.

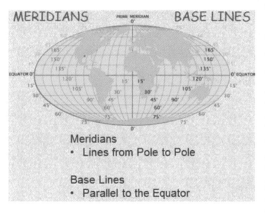

MERIDIANS   PRIME MERIDIAN   **BASE LINES**

Meridians
• Lines from Pole to Pole

Base Lines
• Parallel to the Equator

The Rectangular Survey System uses meridians and base lines. Meridians are the imaginary lines that run from the North Pole to the South Pole. The Prime Meridian runs through the Royal Observatory in Greenwich, England and establishes the position of zero degrees longitude. All of the rest of the imaginary meridians are described either East or West of the Prime Meridian.

Base Lines are the imaginary lines that run horizontally around the globe and are parallel to the Equator which establishes the position of zero degrees latitude. All the rest of the imaginary baselines are described either North or South of the Equator.

When the government made the decision to open an area of land for settlement, the first step was to survey the entire area to be disposed of and assign a description to identify each parcel of land to be sold or granted. Using the PLSS – Rectangular Survey System, the land that was being disposed of was placed on a large grid with every square of the grid being individually identified.

In order to further simplify the system, the government added more identifier Meridians and Baselines in between those longitudinal and latitudinal imaginary lines. Some states have more than one Meridian and Base line if different areas of land were opened at different times. For example Mississippi has five.

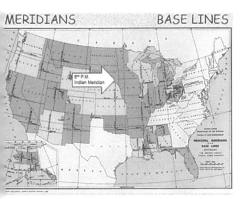

MERIDIANS   BASE LINES

The Meridians and Baselines were given names to help identify where they were. Some examples: the 6th Principal Meridian is also the Indian Meridian and runs N/S through Oklahoma, the Louisiana Meridian runs N/S through Louisiana; the Huntsville Meridian runs N/S through Alabama. And the 1807 Baseline runs E/W at the southern edge of Tennessee and north of Alabama; the 1815 Baseline runs E/W through the center of Arkansas and the 1870 Baseline runs E/W through Oklahoma. A web address for a complete list of Meridians and Base lines is in the Reference Section of this guide.

In the Rectangular Survey System, a TOWNSHIP is usually* six (6) miles by six (6) miles square, 36 square miles, and is measured to the NORTH or to the SOUTH of the predetermined Baseline.

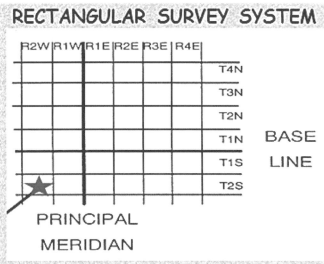

RANGE: E/W of Meridian; each 6 miles wide
TOWNSHIP: N/S of Base Line; each 6 miles wid

The first six miles NORTH of the predetermined Baselin is Township One North written T 1 N, running from 0 t 6 miles North of the Baseline.

RANGE measures EAST or WEST from th predetermined Principal Meridian. Ranges are als usually six miles square in size. The first six miles WES of the Principal Meridian would be Range One Wes written R 1 W.

EACH SQUARE in the Rectangular Survey System, SIX MILES BY SIX MILES, IS CALLED A TOWNSHIP. So, in this example, the township where the star is positioned would be described as T2S and R2W, spelled out Township 2 South and Range 2 West". In other words, the second township south of a certain baseline and the second range west of a certain principal meridian.

*Because the survey lines are two dimensional and the earth is spherical, periodic adjustments are made. So not all sections are a perfect square mile or all townships a perfect 36 square miles.

Inside each six mile by six mile Township is further divided into one mile squares called Sections. The numbers in this example shows how the Sections within a Township are numbered.

36	31	32	33	34	35	36	31
80 Ch.			6 Miles — 480 Chains			80 Ch.	80 Ch.
	1 Mile						
1	6	5	4	3	2	1	6
12	7	8	9	10	11	12	7
13	18	17	16	15	14	13	18
24	19	20	21	22	23	24	19
25	30	29	28	27	26	25	30
36	31	32	33	34	35	36	31
1	6	5	4	3	2	1	6

480 Chains — 6 Miles

T.Y.S.   2

Section 1 is always the North East corner section, Section 36 is always the South East corner section of the Township.

Section 16, in the middle of the Township, and Section 36 were reserved for school purposes. The intention was to guarantee that community school houses would be centrally located for all children.

Some Township maps can be found on-line, see the Reference Section of this guide.

Current Township maps can be found in the local county courthouse in the clerk's office, or the register of deeds office, or the county tax department office.

These maps were printed at various intervals through the years as dictated by each individual county. The older maps might also be located on that county web site, in the state archives, through the local genealogy society or even at a major university. It takes time and effort to locate some of the old maps; but they are worth the effort.

Each Section within each Township is one mile by one mile square and contains 640 acres.

When the government surveyed the land they broke each section down into quarters - assigning the N, S, E, W reference to the quarters. As property is sold each of these quarters may (and usually is) broken down into smaller and smaller parcels, with all parcels keeping the N, S, E, W designations and the fraction amount of the whole section. Land can be surveyed into a variety of land squares or rectangles within each section.

Legal descriptions of land surveyed using the Rectangular Survey System are pretty cut and dried. Within a specific County and State, the legal descriptions give the location within the section, the NW ¼, the NE ¼, etc., the section number, township, and range. For example, the E ½ of Lot 8, of the NE ¼ , S2, T34N, R29W .. spelled out - the East one-half of Lot Number Eight of the North East quarter located in Section 2, Township 34 North, and Range 29 West.

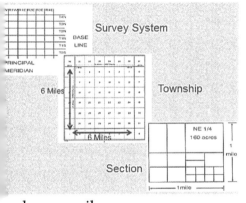

RECAP:

- Townships in the Rectangular Survey System are 6 miles by 6 miles
- Each section within each township is one mile by one mile

Sections can be divided into even smaller plots

IMPORTANT: In states using the Rectangular Survey System (PLSS), even if a county's boundary lines changed, **the legal description of the land did not change!** In other words, THE SECTION, TOWNSHIP, RANGE AND MERIDIAN THAT WERE SET AT THE LAND OPENING ARE THE SAME ONES IN USE TODAY.

Once a researcher has the range and principal meridian boundaries of the Township in which their ancestors lived and the legal description of the land, it is a relatively easy matter to locate the land using a current map.

Chapter 5

The Census

From this point in this land records guide, I am going to demonstrate using my Great-Grandfather, Issac 'Ike' Hollister's farming migration from Missouri into Oklahoma for a government land grant and then retiring back to Missouri.

The starting place for any researcher interested in finding ancestors must begin with the United States or individual state Census records.

Beginning with 1850, the US Census records listed all members of the household. Some individual states further decided to count its citizens on the off US Census five-year time frames. A researcher can find an ancestor at least every ten years and in certain states every five years.

Townships were listed on U S Census

TWELFTH CENSUS OF THE UNITED STATES.

SCHEDULE No. 1.—POPULATION.

DATE	
STATE	Missouri
COUNTY	Vernon County
TOWNSHIP	Montevallo Township

The Census records also recorded the date the Census was taken, the state and county where it was taken and, the TOWNSHIP

NAME where the Census was taken.

In this US Census taken in 1900, Ike Hollister resided in Missouri, Vernon County and Montevallo Township. The TOWNSHIP NAME is the key to finding ancestor's land.

Rectangular Survey Township and Range **Numbers** were NOT listed on the individual Census page. So the researcher must start with the Township by NAME and GO FIND the Township Number and Range Number.

TAKE HEART! At this point, a genealogy researcher has located their ancestor's land within about a six mile area!

Chapter 6

A Visit to the County Courthouse

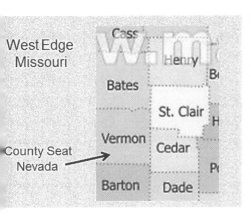

Starting with the state map, the researcher can locate the county, as in this example: the US Census showed Isaac Hollister lived in Missouri in Vernon County.

The local county courthouse will be located at the county seat, which in Vernon County, Missouri is the town of Nevada.

Side note: Your research will be more satisfying if you take some items along with you when you visit the courthouse. Dress comfortably, including shoes. At a minimum, take:

- Your research list of items you hope to find. Include dates, all possible surnames, and TOWNSHIP name.
- Pencils/pens and a note book or writing tablet. Keep good records of what you have already searched.
- Laptop, tablet, or cell phone. You will want to be able to take pictures of documents.

At this point, the researcher has only identified the Township by Name and must determine the Range and Principal Meridian associated with that Township name, so it's time to visit the County Courthouse.

In most County courthouses in one of their departments, there exists a large book, called a Tract Book. This book lists BY TOWNSHIP NAME all of the Townships within that county. On this Tract of Vernon County, Missouri one can count 20 Townships and the Township names are printed on the Tract.

Some counties keep the Tract Book in the County Clerk's office, some keep it with a Register of Deeds, and almost all counties have a current Tract Book in its Tax Department. In addition, a researcher might find tracts on county websites, in state archives, at major universities and in genealogical society libraries.

The Tract Book is divided first into sections by Range Numbers and within the Range by Townships Numbers and within Townships by Section Numbers.

By looking at the tract of a specific county, a researcher can identify the location of the Township BY THE NAME that was listed on the Census record, and consequently identify WITHIN ABOUT SIX MILES where his ancestor lived.

Remember, the boundaries are not always EXACTLY six miles by six miles. There are sometimes variances due to the geographic lay-out of the land.

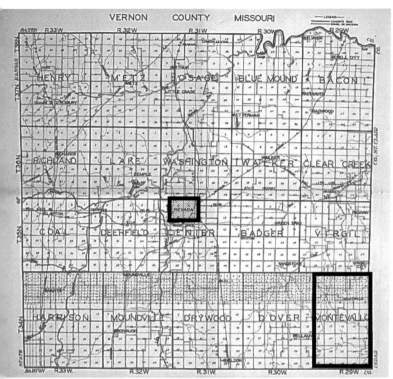

n keeping with Issac Hollister's land location, the esearcher can see that Montevallo Township is located 1 the Southeast corner of Vernon County, about six 1iles south and about eleven miles east of Nevada, the ounty seat. It is located at T34N and R29W, spelled out, ownship 34 North and Range 29 West.

1 the same Tract Book where the whole county Tract is cated single pages of each Township can be found.

'ld Township maps sometimes can be found, depending n how a specific county chooses to keep its files. The esearcher on occasion can find a map of the individual ownship for a given date in time, and sometimes discover their ancestor on a map, BY NAME. This is an exciting document for most researchers.

Missouri
Vernon County
Montevallo TWP
T34N
R29W 1908

Sections 1, 12, 13, 24, 29, and 36 were in Cedar County, Missouri, Benton TWP

http://www.earthpoint.us/Townships.aspx

Montevallo Township is a good example of how townships are sometimes located in two different counties. This map included ONLY Vernon County and in order to add Sections 1, 12, 13, 24, 25, and 36, a map of Montevallo Township in Cedar County, Missouri must be obtained. have sketched them onto this picture of Vernon County Montevallo Township.

Although the property may have started in one county and ended up in another (or even in an adjoining state the individual legal descriptions have not changed. A counties were formed from existing counties the count lines normally followed the section or township lines, bu not always. Most county tax assessor offices have map that show the sections, townships and ranges within thei county. Some counties have actual road maps that show at least the townships and ranges. Contact the Ta Assessor's office in your county of interest about th availability of these types of maps.

The next step is to search in the individual Land Record books for the specific Land Record.

Register of Deeds or County Clerk

Some counties have filmed the Land Records onto microfilm. However, other counties allow researchers to search through the actual Land Record books. The Land Record books are found either in the County Clerk's office or with the Register of Deeds and date back to the beginning of when records were kept for that county.

Record books at courthouses are large and heavy. Most weigh about 15-20 pounds. They are "racked" on metal shelves with "pockets" sized to contain these large books. Each pocket has a set of rollers that help the book to slide in and out. These racks sometimes reach from the floor to ceiling.

The deed books are in chronological order. Within these books are recorded all deeds, claims, patents, leases, security (trust) deeds, mortgages, bonds, quit claim deeds, liens filed against land, and tax deeds. In addition, the researcher can find other records such as court cases, adoptions, and a multitude of other legal documentation in books located in these rooms.

Most county courthouses record rooms are crowded, cramped and dusty. There are usually other people working in the record rooms, doing title searches for current land sales. The genealogists must understand that the work of the clerk or registrar is to provide documents for current land sales and must spend their work day in those pursuits. However, the clerks will usually help the genealogy researcher when they can spare the time.

It is hard work to pull the books out, find the page you want, haul it to the photo copy machine, or scan it with a portable scanner, haul it back and re-rack it. Take someone along to help you.

The search is most fruitful if the researcher has done his homework prior to making the trip to the courthouse and brings to the courthouse a list of all possible dates of residence, last names, maiden names, etc., that the researcher has discovered, and is prepared to look through the index for any, and all the possible date and name combinations.

Early counties recorded an index in the front of individual deed books. Later on, counties began using a Master Index Book. The Master Index is divided in two (2) sections. The front section lists the seller (grantor) and followed immediately by a second section listing the buyer (grantee). The grantor and grantee sections are further divided in alphabetical sections.

The transactions (deed, patent, lease, etc.) are listed in the ORDER they were brought to the courthouse for the purpose of recording. The recorder listed the deed on the next blank line in the alphabetical section that corresponds to the FIRST LETTER OF THE SELLER'S LAST NAME.

You can see Issac Hollister's name listed here on Feb 12, 897. To the right of his name, the court recorder listed the individual deed book number and the page number where the actual deed is recorded. The same information is recorded for the Seller, J. M. Crain in the seller section of the Master Index.

BY YEAR, ALPHABETICAL INDEX
By Grantor: Seller
By Grantee: Buyer

side note for further understanding, ANY real estate

descriptor word using OR or EE as its extender refers to the giver of something and the receiver of something.

> Grantor = Seller – the 'giver' of the land
> Grantee = Buyer – the 'receiver' of the land
>
> Mortgagor = Borrower – the 'giver' of the mortgage on land; the land owner
> Mortgagee = Lender - the 'receiver' of the mortgage; they hold a mortgage on the land
>
> Lessor – Landlord – the 'giver' of the lease
> Lessee – Tenant – the 'receiver' of the lease

This practice of using OR and EE holds true in every real estate descriptor word.

Chapter 7

The Land Record

The next step is to find the actual deed book and page for the recorded Homestead Claim, Grant, Patent, or Deed.

HOMESTEAD CLAIM – Documentation of an individual applying to the government to claim ownership of certain acreage.

GRANT – A gift of land made by the government as a reward, especially in return for military service.

PATENT- A record of the initial transfer of land titles from the government to an individual. Many patents can be found on-line with the Bureau of Land Management.

DEEDS: The bulk of land records consist of deeds which transfer ownership of land from a seller to a buyer.

The land record contains: the date of the deed, names of the seller(s), buyer(s), a legal description of the property, the amount of money (or equivalent or reason) changing hands, the signature of the seller(s), the date the seller signed the deed and the signatures of witnesses.

Generally, the Master Deed Index record is in the name of only the PRIMARY Seller or Buyer.

Occasionally there is a notation indicating there were other Sellers or Buyers involved. ALL THE NAMES WILL ALL BE ENUMERATED ON THE DEED, even though only the primary seller or buyer is listed in the index.

A wealth of information can be found on the recorded land record: brothers, sisters, their spouses, deceased persons, family friend witnessing to the land record. A researcher should scan every record in the deed books that cover the time frame an ancestor was in the county. Here is another example where it takes time and effort to locate these old items but they are frequently worth the effort.

In the Rectangular Survey System, the legal description consists of Township NUMBER, Range NUMBER and Section or portion of Section NUMBER. The legal description does not usually use the Township Name within the description.

The legal description describes the land. It is made up of the combination of the location within a section, the section number and the range number.

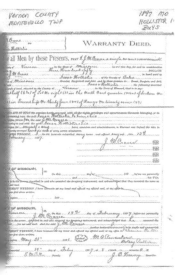

Issac's deed read *"the E ½ of Lot 8, of the NE1/4, S2, T34S, R29W"* Spelled out - the East one-half of Lot Number Eight of the North East quarter located in Section 2, Township 34 South, Range 29 West. His property would be located in the north east corner of Section 2 of this township.

Remember, the identifiers (numbers) of sections, townships and ranges have not changed from when the land was originally surveyed up to and including today. They remain stable.

Chapter 8

Map to the Ancestor's Land

'or each section (one mile by one mile) the land owners of the individual pieces of property are listed.

According to the deed, Ike Hollister owned 40 acres located in the E ½ of Lot 8, of the NE1/4, S2, T34S, R29W . spelled out - the East one-half of Lot Number Eight of the North East quarter located in Section 2, Township 34 outh, Range 29 West.

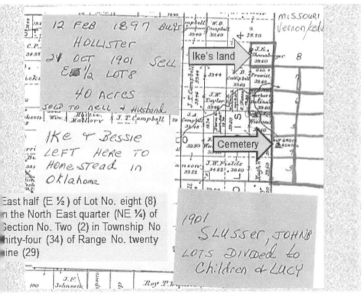

found the copy of both the County Map with all ownships and the individual Montevallo Township Map at the courthouse in Nevada, Missouri. You can see y my notes on this Section Map. Ike bought this land in

1897, he sold it in 1901, where it was located, who he sold it to (a cousin on the other side of my family). In addition, I have noted a paternal uncle's land located in Montevallo Township, but in Cedar County, Missouri. His name was John B. Slusser.

Southeast corner. From here, ¼ N, then ½ mile West, then ¼ miles South, then ½ mile East, back to this corner

With this section Map, and comparing it to a current map of Vernon County, was able to find Ike's property.

What a thrill when I was able to actually walk on Ike's land.

Lewis's Birthplace

House where Grandpa was born in 1885

1940

2012

Using the deed and its legal description and a current map I found the house where Ike's children were born. It is still standing, albeit in a state of disrepair. A family member had taken a photo of the house in 1940, and I took another picture in 2012

Cemeteries are frequently noted on Tracts. I discovered the Walnut Grove School and Cemetery were located on that paternal uncle Slusser's land and that several family members are buried in this cemetery.

1910 US Census
Oklahoma
Harper County
Kiowa Township

In 1901 Ike traveled by covered wagon into Oklahoma Territory. This 1910 US Census shows that Ike Hollister and his family resided in Harper County, Oklahoma Kiowa Township. I knew that they homesteaded in klahoma and this Census gives me documentation of eir location.

trip to the Harper County Courthouse in Buffalo, klahoma produced the County and Township Tract aps.

ne Buffalo County Courthouse was a treasure chest of ocuments for my family history. Both of my Great

Grandfather's homesteaded in Harper County, Oklahoma and their children met and married there. That's my family history! I will only concentrate on information for Ike Hollister for this guide.

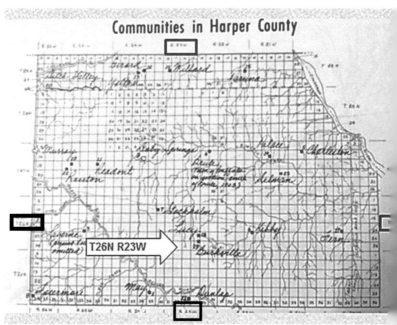

Communities in Harper County

The Tract Map of Harper County, Oklahoma does NOT list the individual names of Townships. However, the Township Numbers and Range Numbers are listed.

(RECORD OF PATENTS.)
4-404-177.

The United States of America,

Be all to whom these presents shall come, Greeting:

Homestead Certificate No. 5691.

Application 10466.

WHEREAS, There has been deposited in the GENERAL LAND OFFICE of the United States a Certificate of the Register of the Land Office at Woodward, Oklahoma, whereby it appears that, pursuant to the Act of Congress approved 20th May, 1862, "To secure Homesteads to Actual Settlers on the Public Domain," and the acts supplemental thereto, the claim of ISAAC K. HOLLISTER

has been established and duly consummated, in conformity to law, for the north half of the northwest quarter and the north half of the northeast quarter of Section thirty-four in Township twenty-six north of Range twenty-three west of the Indian Meridian, Oklahoma, containing one hundred sixty acres,

according to the Official Plat of the Survey of the said Land, returned to the GENERAL LAND OFFICE by the Surveyor General:

NOW KNOW YE, That there is, therefore, granted by the UNITED STATES unto the said Isaac K. Hollister

the tract of Land above described; TO HAVE AND TO HOLD the said tract of Land, with the appurtenances thereof, unto the said Isaac K. Hollister

and to his heirs and assigns forever.

IN TESTIMONY WHEREOF, I, Theodore Roosevelt , President of the United States of America, have caused these letters to be made Patent, and the seal of the General Land Office to be hereunto affixed.

(SEAL) GIVEN under my hand, at the City of Washington, the _____twenty-fourth_____ day of _____February____, in the year of our Lord one thousand nine hundred and _____eight_____, and of the Independence of the United States the one hundred and ____thirty-second____.

By the President: *Theodore Roosevelt*

By _____ *M. W. Young.* Secretary.

_____
Recorder of the General Land Office.

The patent issued in 1908 records that Ike Hollister homesteaded on and gained ownership of

"the north half of the northwest quarter and the north half of the northeast quarter of Section 34 in Township 26 North and Range 23 West of the Indian Meridian, Oklahoma, containing one hundred sixty acres".

PATENT- A record of the initial transfer of land titles from the government to an individual. Many patents can be found on-line with the Bureau of Land Management. See the website for the BLM in the Reference Section of this guide.

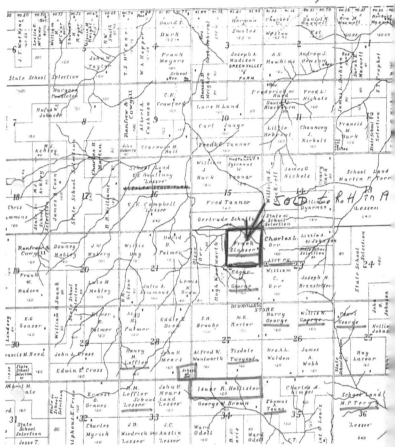

14-JUL-1911 OK
SLUSSER, Richard H.

The Tract Map of Township 26 North and Range 23 West
printed in 1905 showed the Sections and the **first settler**
who claimed the land. Both of my Great Grandfather
are listed along with their neighbors, whose names I saw
recorded on the 1910 US Census.

Ike's land today

Using a current Harper County Map, I could match enough land marks and local roads that I could map my route out to Ike's land.

I was able to walk Ike's Oklahoma land. The current owner went with my brother and me and we were able to find a number of locations where Ike may have built his dug-out.

Once again, schools, cemeteries and post offices are frequently listed on the Tract Maps.

Pleasant Grove School-Ike's daughter attended

You can see where the local school was located catty-corner North and West from Ike's land in South East corner of Section 28. I discovered the school Ike's daughter Josie and the younger of the Slusser children attended.

Chapter 9

The Plat Map; Lot and Block System

The **Plat Map system** uses Lot numbers and Block numbers in a contiguously improved acreage, called a development. It is probably the most easily understood of the three main land records systems. The Plat also lists the Subdivision Name and the county and state where the subdivision is located.

When cities began to expand into surrounding farmland, owners of a large tract of land would create a plat and subdivide the tract into a series of smaller lots to be sold to buyers. They recorded the plat with the city or county. The plat map would then be the basis for all the lots in the subdivision and together make up the legal descriptions. The legal description is recorded on each deed.

Ike Hollister resided in Oklahoma from about 1902 until he sold his land in 1914 and retired back to Missouri.

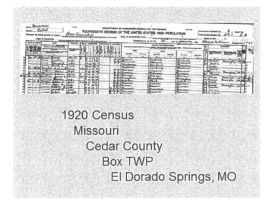

1920 Census
Missouri
Cedar County
Box TWP
El Dorado Springs, MO

According to the 1920 US Census, Ike's final land ownership was located in the town of El Dorado Springs, Cedar County, and Box Township, Missouri. The Census shows he lived on 1st Street in El Dorado Springs.

A trip to the Cedar County Courthouse in Stafford, Missouri produced Ike's deed and a copy of the Summer's Addition to El Dorado Springs plat map.

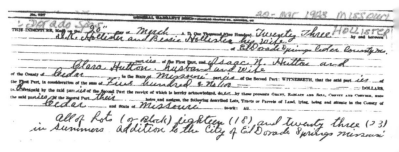

Ike Hollister's 1923 deed records that he bought All of Lots Eighteen (18) and Twenty three (23) of Summer's Addition to the City of El dorado Springs, Missouri

Summer's Addition.

sing the Summer's Addition Plat Map, I can see where ots 18 and 23 are and follow the map to Ike's lots. The ensus listed Ike and Bessie on 1st Street. Their house robably faced West on Lot 18, facing 1st Street.

he Township and Range coordinates are on this plat ap. They are "Summer's Addition to the original town lat of Eldorado Springs is estimated on and consists of e SE NE and the NE SE also 10 acres off the East Side of E SE and 10 acres off the East side of the NW SE all in ction 20 Township 36 Range 28 W of the fifth principal eridian and consists of lots and streets as set forth in e above plat".

This house is no longer there. By Bessie's apparent age in this photo, I assume this was one of their last residences. I did view the lots as they appear today. I cannot express the thrill it is to actually stand on the street in front of the lots in El Dorado Springs, Missouri where Ike and Bessie lived, and eventually died.

They are buried in El Dorado Springs, Missouri Cemetery.

Rest in peace, Issac K. and Mina Elizabeth 'Bessie' Hollister.

CONCLUSION

Researchers: Don't be satisfied with just a visit to the grave of your ancestors. Since you are already at the site where they passed away, you are probably where they lived last. Take a walk where they walked. See what they saw. Picture what their life might have been like. You do not have to avoid county courthouses because you might think the information there is too complicated, or hard to find. The process is time-consuming, but relatively easy.

Do your homework first to avoid a frustrating trip to the courthouse. Starting with the governmental Census records

- Determine date, state, county, TOWNSHIP and post office
- Visit the appropriate county courthouse
  - o Get a copy of land tract of the COUNTY
  - o Get a copy of the TOWNSHIP map
  - o Search the Deed Index Book
  - o Locate the Land Record
- Map route to ancestor's land.
- Go for a walk on that land

You will be glad you did! Good luck to you! HAPPY FOOTSTEPS!!

RESOURCES AND HELPFUL WEBSITES

Staff (May 29, 2012) *The Public Land Survey System* (PLSS). National Atlas of the United States. U.S. Department of the Interior. Retrieved June 20, 2012.

http://www.earthpoint.us/Townships.aspx   Uses Google Point to display Township, Range and sometimes ¼ sections

http://www.worldatlas.com/aatlas/imageg.htm   National Atlas of Township and Range

Haas-Davenport, Linda. *Taking the Mystery out of Land Records*. 2006 http://www.lhaasdav.com/

White, C. Albert (1983)   *A History of the Rectangular Survey System (PLSS)*. Washington D.; Bureau of Land Management. P. 115 OCLC http: //www.worldcat.org

Utterback, William, Certified Genealogist http://users.arn.net/billco/uslpr.htm   Lessons on US Land & Property Research

www.Familysearch.org   List of available microfilmed records

http://www.usgenweb.org States and counties within the US have websites containing all sorts of historical and genealogical information.

http://www.glorecords.blm.gov/ Access to Federal land conveyance records in states using the Township, Range Section Survey method. More than five MILLION records issued from 1820 to the present. DOES NOT contain EVERY state. Resource links for most states.

http://www.glorecords.blm.gov/Visitors/PrincipleMeridiansAndBaselines.html A **map of US** meridians and baselines

http://www.ancestry.com **Red Book: American State County, and Town Sources** Among other things each book contains maps of each state laid out by current counties. Information on the dates each county was formed and inclusive dates of land records held at the county courthouse.

http://www.everton.com **The Handy Book For Genealogists**. Among other things, boundary changes that took place over time. Everton Publishers' PO Box 368, Logan, Utah 84323-0368

http://en.wikipedia.org/wiki/Longitude Describes Meridians and Baselines